Energetic Perspectives

A Soul Essence Art Exploration {SEA} In-the-Round Coloring & Adult Activity Book

© 2015, 2025 Dawn Richerson
All rights reserved

Energetic Perspectives

*A Soul Essence Art Exploration
{SEA} In-the-Round Coloring
& Adult Activity Book*

Art & Soul Publishing
An Imprint of Soul Simple Innovation LLC

This book may not be reproduced in whole or in part, without written permission from the author, except by a reviewer who may quote brief passages. Nor may any part of this book be reproduced, stored in a retrieval system, or transmitted in any form or by any means electronic, mechanical, photocopying, recording, scanning or otherwise.

ISBN 978-1-942969-84-6

Printed in the United States of America

AUTHOR WEBSITE
www.DawnRicherson.com

Introduction

THIS SOUL ESSENCE ART EXPLORATION and coloring activity book is for any and all who would embrace healing and wholeness, heart-centered expression and radiant expansion from within. The thirty SEA Symbols invite your unique exploration of your essential self, journey, and truth. Draw on your soul's deep knowing as you engage with the symbols in this collection. Each image is a seed for life that offers an energetic perspective of life's unfolding mystery in this, our time of great transformation.

Consider soul-activating starter questions with SEEDS Journaling Practice for the Soulful Exploration for the Essential Discovery of the Self. Allow them to connect you to the questions and the story of life that is alive in you. Prepare for the movement of life energy associated with each symbol. Then, add color and your own soul doodles alongside essential notes and journal entries that respond to what arises.

Use the *Energetic Perspectives* coloring and activity book to connect more deeply with your soul's knowing and intuition as you explore life movements that can support you as you come to LIFE and Live In Full Expression. Begin within, exploring patterns of potentiality revealed within whole worlds of wonder.

These energetic patterns emanate from the heart and soul of who we are and are reflected in the world around us. They extend an invitation to the dance of your life. Follow the flow of your soul's deepest knowing. Allow the colors of your life's experience onto the page, using colored pencils, crayons, markers or a paintbrush to find the clearing within you and create from this space. Become a soul explorer as you make your way through a month's worth of soul explorations. See beauty. Touch wonder. Dance with mystery as you form, re-form, and trans-form your own energetic perspectives.

I trust this playful book of my own Soul Essence Art {SEA} doodles will reconnect you to you—to the light, life, and love you are at your core. This is the joy of my own life's work. We begin and we begin again, ever evolving and expanding from the whole of who we are. I wish you deep joy as you engage with these energetic perspectives in the round. **DAWN RICHERSON**

Ancient Echo

Down through the ages, far across galaxies of time and from the depths of space, emerges the ancient echo. We must be still to hear the resounding truth that reverberates in the core of our being. Listen for what is most true, and speak with your true voice.

SEEDS Journaling Practice: *Soul Activation Quest-ions to Consider*

➡ What distant "memories" call to you?

➡ In the layers of influence and opinion, what is true to your unique voice?

➡ How might you learn to listen for and distinguish your own ancient echo?

➡ How does your authentic voice echo an ancient truth?

➡ Gazing into your interpretation of this SEA doodle, what questions arise from within? Record them here and explore further.

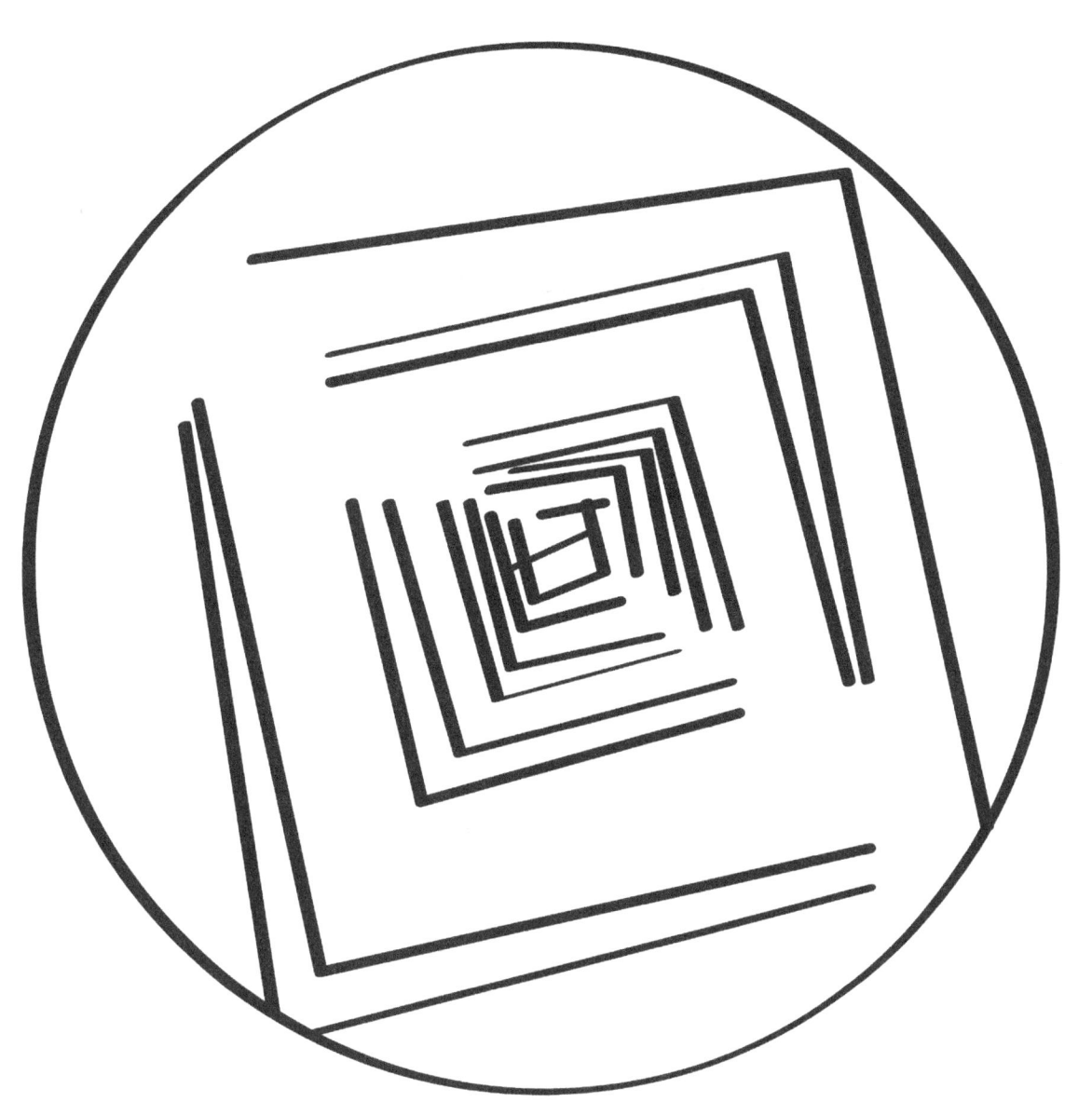

Attuned

Within the structure of your being, there is a song that rises from your soul. Its singular signature is yours alone. The harmony that emanates from this threefold convergence of the light, life, and love you are awakens world upon worlds within. Attune yourself to the frequencies only you know as "true" and watch in amazement the universal dance of all creation begin anew.

SEEDS Journaling Practice: *Soul Activation Quest-ions to Consider*

- Do you see, feel, or hear energetic waves or patterns in, around, or through you?
- Day by day, to what harmonies or disharmonies are you most attuned?
- What daily practices would attune you to that which is true for you?
- What is your unique tri-tone foundation?
- Gazing into your interpretation of this SEA doodle, what questions arise from within? Record them here and explore further.

Congregation

We gather, drawn together in higher realms, to explore truths or beliefs. We are called forth, attracted naturally to one another to see where our story goes. The ever-shifting dynamics of our play of light sometimes casts a shadow, sometimes reveals us to be more than who we knew ourselves to be. Consider the gifts and opportunities for growth born from the gathering of souls.

SEEDS Journaling Practice: *Soul Activation Quest-ions to Consider*

➡ Choose one group with which you are affiliated or to which you belong. What dynamics are at play? How can the shadows lead you back to light?

➡ Do I feel so small amidst those who "belong" or constricted by the circle? Or am I expanded into new dimensions and raised to new possibility?

➡ Is there an element of hiding out in the group? Or does being with a gathering of souls bring you to center and ground you in the light, life, and love you are?

➡ Gazing into your interpretation of this SEA doodle, what questions arise from within? Record them here and explore further.

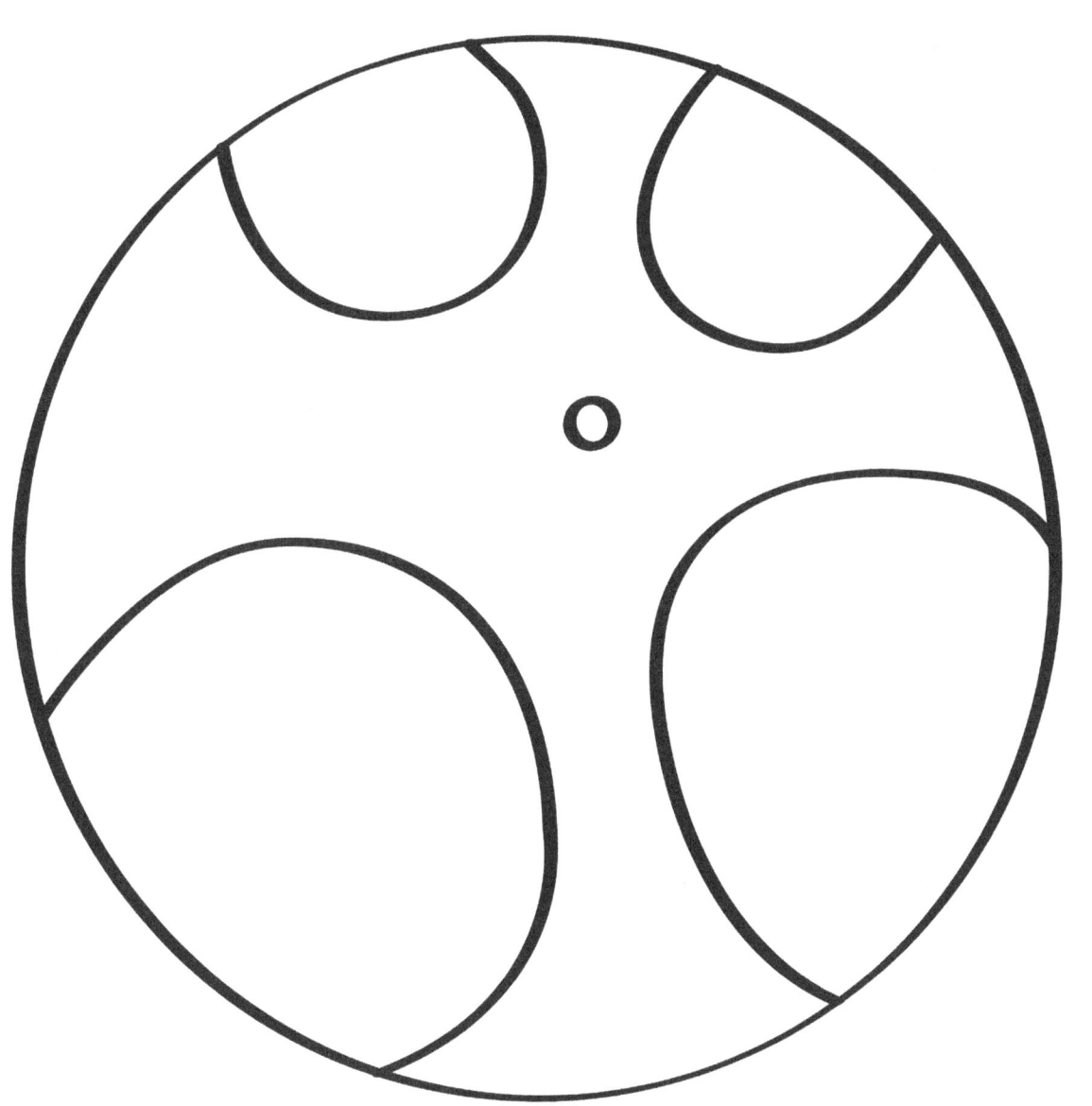

Conical

Without a surface and solid ground of being, form cannot sustain itself. We long for a space to be—a "home" (physical, emotional, or spiritual) and a dwelling place. We create spaces to express something about who we are. Let the spaces into which you enter be consecrated to the nourishment of your soul and the refinement of your life. Let these spaces be receptacles for treasuring your heart's true home. Give thanks for this sacred ground of space and time.

SEEDS Journaling Practice: *Soul Activation Quest-ions to Consider*

- What are the spaces that support you as you grow your soul and share your gifts?
- What "home" do you long for? How might you create that from solid ground?
- What is your heart's true home? How can you invite and express more of your inner knowing about that home into the spaces you inhabit?
- Gazing into your interpretation of this SEA doodle, what questions arise from within? Record them here and explore further.

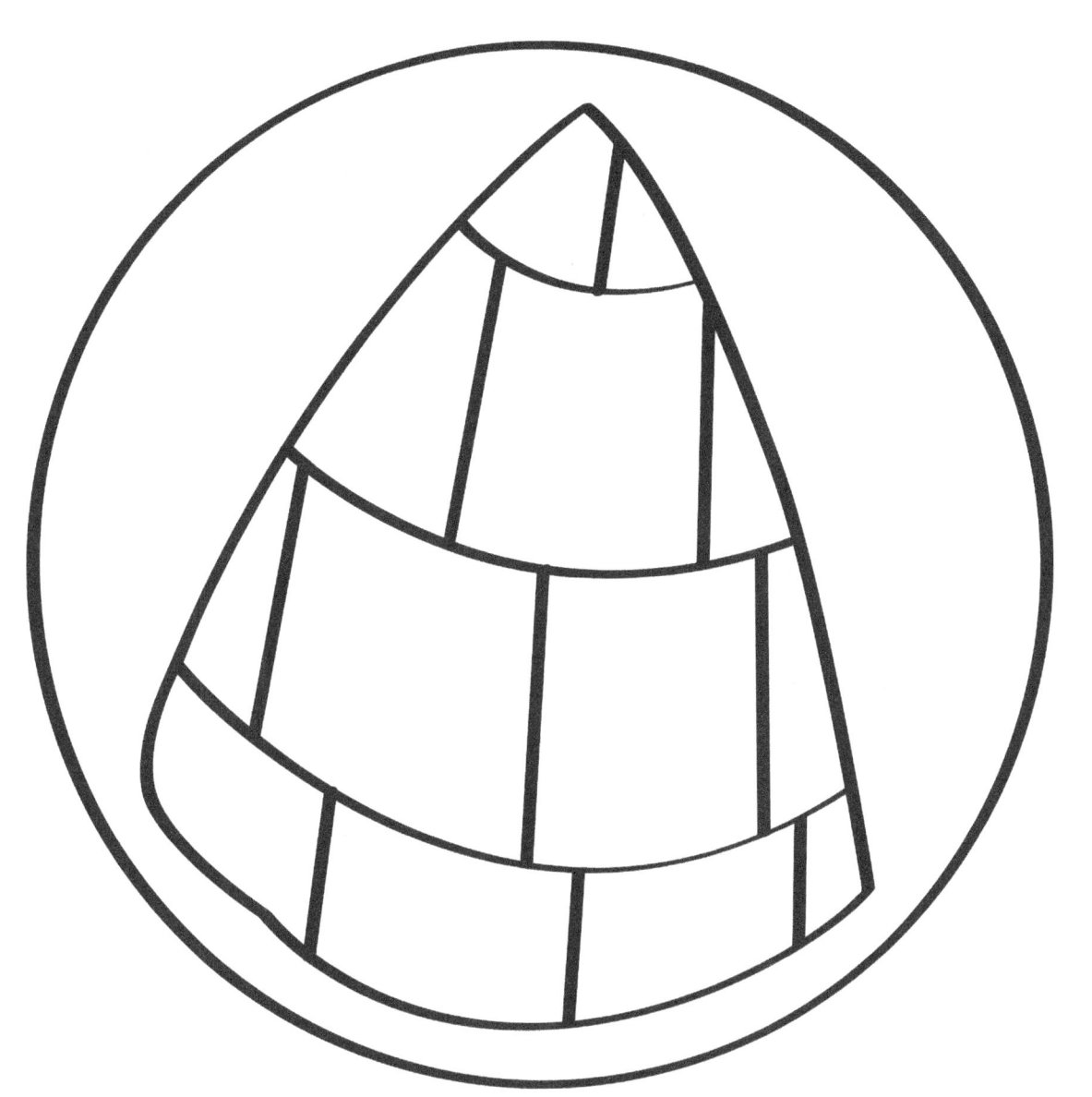

Creative Clash

Sun and moon. Sea and stars. Stillness and the dance of life. We live in a world of contrasts and an infinite variety of expression. How might the chaos and the clash of ideas, truths, and perspectives be an opening for you now?

SEEDS Journaling Practice: *Soul Activation Quest-ions to Consider*

➡ Where in your life are you feeling you must choose one way over another? How do you experience a creative clash within your being?

➡ Is it possible to find a chorus of unity in light of divergent interests and beliefs?

➡ How might you honor another's creative soul expression when it does not fit in neatly to the confines of your worldview? What happens when you do this?

➡ What way of moving through life leads you into joy? How might you make room for more creative expression day by day?

➡ Gazing into your interpretation of this SEA doodle, what questions arise from within? Record them here and explore further.

Differentiation

We are born into the same world. We are one of many souls who share so much. Yet, while the pattern of nature as expressed in a variety of forms—humanity included—is clear, within any group who share a common heritage, home, or hope are individuals arrayed in glorious robes of light, each one a shining original. This differentiation, too, is by design.

SEEDS Journaling Practice: *Soul Activation Quest-ions to Consider*

- What are the ways you are a unique expression of the One Light: your defining characteristics, your fine gifts of original design, and the varieties of your life's essential journey and unique experience, for example?
- What do we all share in common?
- How do you uniquely express truths you share with family groups and circles of belonging?
- How do you express those sacred seeds of essence you alone have come bearing in your soul?
- Gazing into your interpretation of this SEA doodle, what questions arise from within? Record them here and explore further.

Eternal Love

Love is a river that runs through us and through all that is and ever was, and that love takes many forms. You are a form shaped from the eternal heartbeat, invited into experience. Will you pass through the gate of Love's eternal flame and know what you know?

SEEDS Journaling Practice: *Soul Activation Quest-ions to Consider*

➡ Do you hold the Love you are within a heart made to be a fortress?
Or do you allow that love to radiate without and within, moving in infinite directions through all time and space?

➡ How have you experienced a love that is endless and infinite? What action might you take or practice might you adopt to step into a greater Love that feeds your life and leads you to a higher, deeper, truer experience of you?

➡ What gate are you invited to pass through as you enter Love's portal of truth and infinite belonging? What flames burn forever?

➡ Gazing into your interpretation of this SEA doodle, what questions arise from within? Record them here and explore further.

Expanded Dimensions

Life, when we enter fully into it, stretches us. We are expanded into new patterns of being. Experiences we like just the way they are can be rearranged without warning by the free choice of those who share this space and time. Everything changes. Yet, magically and sometimes miraculously, the center not only holds; it grows. It becomes. And, then, when we are ready, it returns to the mysterious whole that knows no beginning and is without end.

SEEDS Journaling Practice: *Soul Activation Quest-ions to Consider*

➡ What do you see when you look for yourself? What has changed? What has remained ever the same? Who are you now?

➡ How have the shifting experiences of your life expanded your perspective? How might you consider various layers of truth in any given situation and allow what is to be even as you make room for a miracle?

➡ How does an experience you are now having feel flat or limiting? What are the opportunities for infusing it with expanded thinking or actions that open a space for something more? What if you rested in the knowing that all is well and you are whole?

➡ Gazing into your interpretation of this SEA doodle, what questions arise from within? Record them here and explore further.

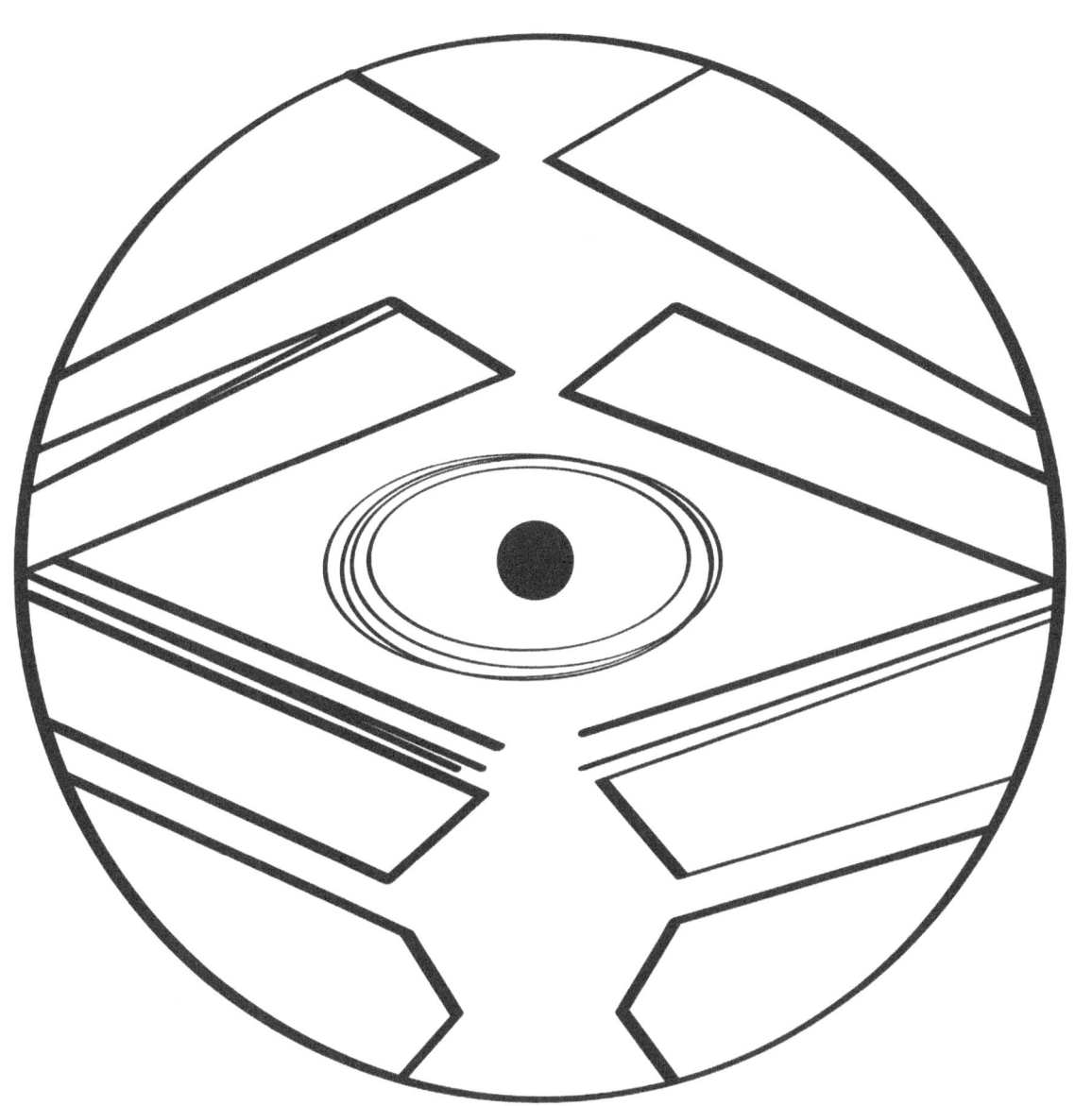

Fish Eye

Often, we get hooked into a particular frame of reference and keep to the rivers we know. We travel in the same circles, never daring to be the fish out of water. This incarnation you chose is an invitation to life's forever flow. Enter into the mystery. Come and see. Swim in the river to see what you can see.

SEEDS Journaling Practice: *Soul Activation Quest-ions to Consider*

- What is your familiar sea? How can you enter into new oceans of experience while holding to the true nature of who you are?

- In your current river of life, what do you know? What do you see? How might you contribute your own interpretation of life's mystery in ways that expand this reality for yourself, for those who swim in the same stream, and for those who have never considered or felt the sense of wonder you have found in the waters of your own experience?

- What does Spirit see when it gazes upon the beauty of who you are?

- Gazing into your interpretation of this SEA doodle, what questions arise from within? Record them here and explore further.

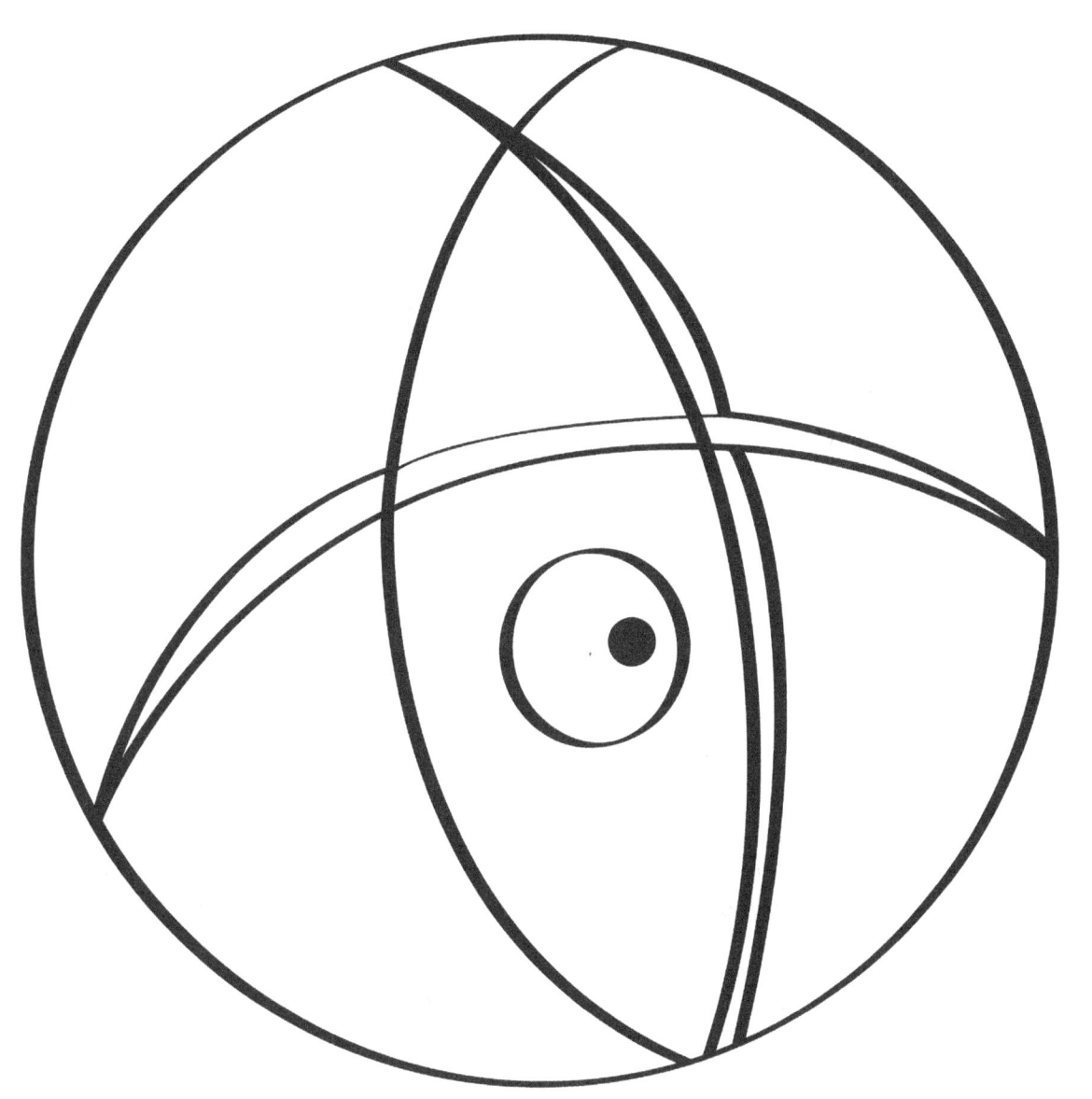

Held in Grace

From Love was born the mother of this world, and the world itself is an expression of her gracious presence. Your world and your life are the seeds she holds with loving care. Yours are the wings unfurled. Yours is the comfort of her song and also the song she loves the most. Held within the sphere of tenderness, we are born, again and again, to light, to life, to love. In those moments when we experience a dying or a falling away, we are met along the way, gathered up and held in an infinite grace.

SEEDS Journaling Practice: *Soul Activation Quest-ions to Consider*

➡ What does "grace" mean to you? When you look back at your life, how have you experienced grace? What was its source? How were you held within it?

➡ In what ways do you see that your sacred seeds of essence are held in grace?

➡ How are you currently being born again to life or letting go of something that no longer leads you into life? In what way might you rest in grace?

➡ Gazing into your interpretation of this SEA doodle, what questions arise from within? Record them here and explore further.

Infinite Dimensions

The exploration into all begins with the universal seed of the desire for life and the life more abundant. The question sounds as a heartbeat, steady and true, playfully inviting us into something beyond the ordinary and mundane. Who would you be? What edges might you explore? What wonders would you know in this world of form held within the ever-expanding sphere?

SEEDS Journaling Practice: *Soul Activation Quest-ions to Consider*

- What do you dream of? What is your desired experience? What life might you try on for size, exploring an expression of your particular seed of life?

- Do you limit your life with a particular circumference, defined by your choice to stay put at a single center point?

- In the dance of your life, do you allow yourself room to grow? Do you see to infinity and beyond, knowing and trusting there is always more?

- Gazing into your interpretation of this SEA doodle, what questions arise from within? Record them here and explore further.

Janus Rising

In the dream of life, we share a memory that we have too often cast aside in our hurry to achieve all we think important. It whispers down through time, inviting us into a new day. Our life is held within the dream we dreamed, and we ourselves are the key to its meaning.

SEEDS Journaling Practice: *Soul Activation Quest-ions to Consider*

→ What memory do you carry? What ancient wisdom do you know?

→ What dreams arise within you? Write down those dreams you have brought fully to life and those that have not yet come to full fruition.

→ Are you listening to your Wise Woman or Wise Warrior Within? What is she or he whispering to you about your life? For what has she or he come to awaken you to so that you might usher in a whole new way forward for the collective?

→ Gazing into your interpretation of this SEA doodle, what questions arise from within? Record them here and explore further.

Life Dance

Today is the day we shine. Tonight's the night. We have come to the dance, and now is the moment. We received an invitation to life's dance the moment we were conceived. In Spirit and in flesh, we were born into this life to be and to become, to express our soul's deep knowing, and to grow in stature and in truth.

SEEDS Journaling Practice: *Soul Activation Quest-ions to Consider*

➡ What unique pattern of life do you bring forward in this time? How do you see that pattern replicated, rippling through the fabric of our collective experience?

➡ Have you been waiting for an invitation to the dance? You are here. It is time. No partner is needed, for you hold within streams of soul infused with a patterned impulse and fine gifts of original design. As you twirl through the years, choosing your steps and the way you want to dance, see all you set in motion.

➡ How are you connected to others in the beautiful dance of your life? Where are the touch points, where your way of being exists in close proximity to another's unique experience?

➡ Gazing into your interpretation of this SEA doodle, what questions arise from within? Record them here and explore further.

Life Dynamic

The free will of others and our own choices in this life mean things change. They are rearranged. We ourselves are a dynamic and sustainable system, free to wander, free to choose, free to spread our wings and soar or remain still, and free to come together or to swim in the seas alone.

SEEDS Journaling Practice: *Soul Activation Quest-ions to Consider*

➡ Is your life dynamic? Are you an expression of life's freedom to choose, dream, and explore?

➡ How do you expand and grow? What daring adventures do you choose as you come fully to your life and live in full expression?

➡ When you choose to be in groups with others on the way, what do you notice? Do you grow by your association? Do you maintain your individual expression or lose yourself to what others would tell you is the truth?

➡ Gazing into your interpretation of this SEA doodle, what questions arise from within? Record them here and explore further.

Life Path

Are you walking in the way of your life? Some of us set off on the way laid out before us as the prescribed way of seeing life and becoming who it is presumed we would become. Life's true path unfolds from being. As we express our true nature, we are naturally led to a way that is our own and opened to greater possibility than we could have imagined.

SEEDS Journaling Practice: *Soul Activation Quest-ions to Consider*

- Where are you going? What truths are you exploring? What dialogue has opened in your life as you have moved through life? What questions have invited you into further exploration and a deeper phase of your life's essential journey?

- What is life's journey as you understand it? Describe the path you know through life, considering the grooves of experience and markers of expansion you have met or anticipate meeting as you stay on your life's path.

- How is the path itself alive? How are you yourself an invitation to a way? How might you put words to that way?

- Gazing into your interpretation of this SEA doodle, what question arises from within? Record them here and explore further.

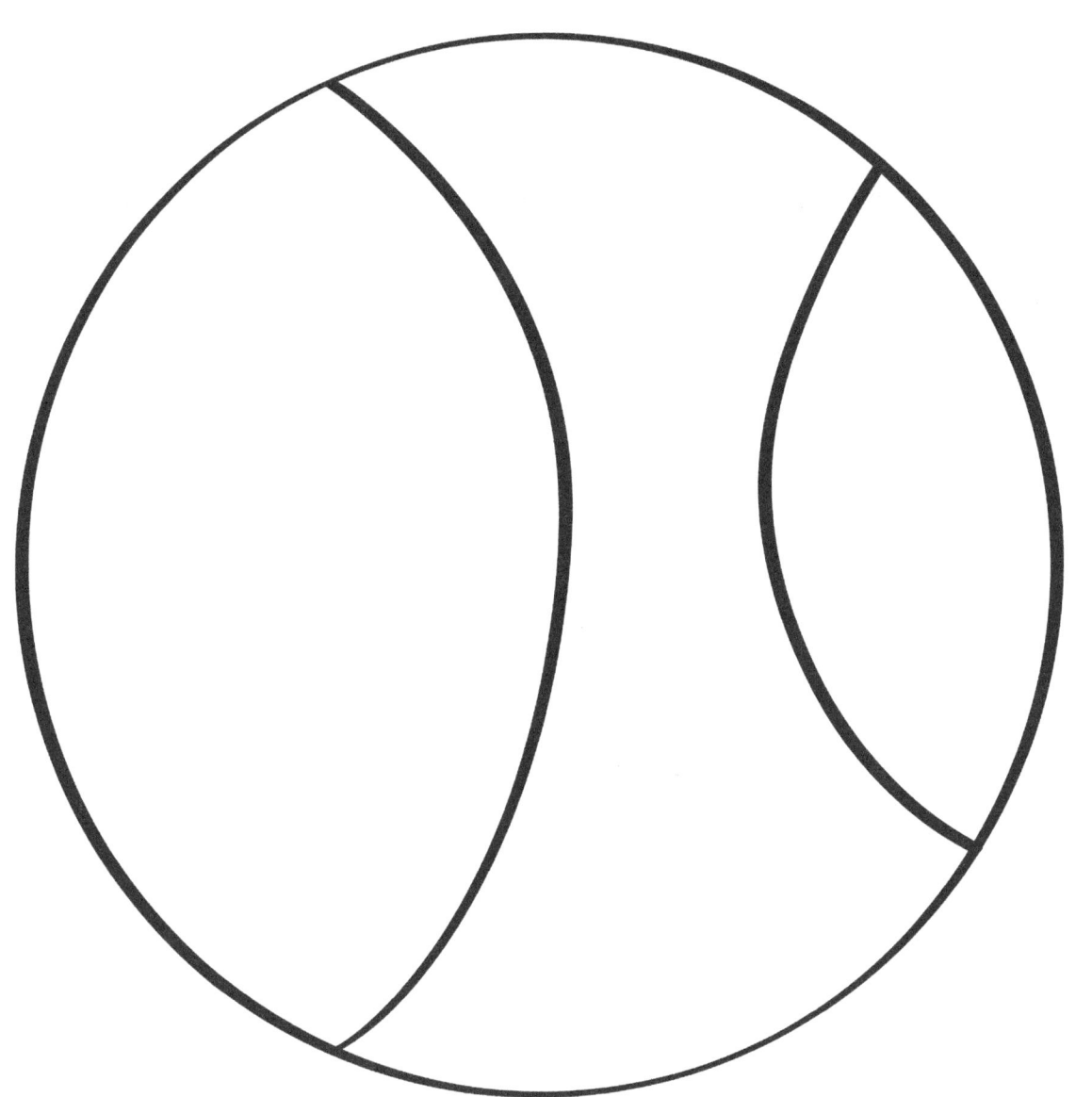

Morpheus

It seems we are moving in a circle. It seems not much is happening. We are happening! We are, step by step, if we choose, becoming the predictable pattern of change that weaves webs of wonder this world has yet to see. Consent to undergo this change, then spread new wings and fly.

SEEDS Journaling Practice: *Soul Activation Quest-ions to Consider*

- Of the thousands of dreams spinning around, which call out most to you? How can you listen to that voice that is an echo of your own and align to it?
- What patterns of life do you create as you are in the process of becoming the fullest expression of who you are?
- What changes are at play in your life right now? What does that feel like to you?
- What is being born or made manifest in you? Through you? With you? For you?
- Gazing into your interpretation of this SEA doodle, what questions arise from within? Record them here and explore further.

Pod

We are vessels, carriers of sacred seeds of essence, entrusted to carry this unique message in a bottle to the world. In the pod of our experience is life's true experiment. So much happens here in these bodies and in the container of the moment, the hour, the day, the year, the single lifetime that is a ship carrying a most precious, life-giving cargo meant to be shared for sustenance and savor. Have you taken a look around to see what's stored in the hold just below deck and the surface of things?

SEEDS Journaling Practice: *Soul Activation Quest-ions to Consider*

➡ Is your pod about to burst or is it hard and shriveled up? How might you water your life, tending to your soul's garden so that it might bear fruit and feed a hungry world?

➡ Are you sailing your vessel, daring to fly your own flag and make your own way? Do you know what it is you carry through this space and time?

➡ What is the journey you have chosen to make? What are the ports where you will rest awhile and share your seeds for life and life-giving water with those who thirst, who have not tasted all so graciously been bestowed upon you?

➡ Gazing into your interpretation of this SEA doodle, what questions arise from within? Record them here and explore further.

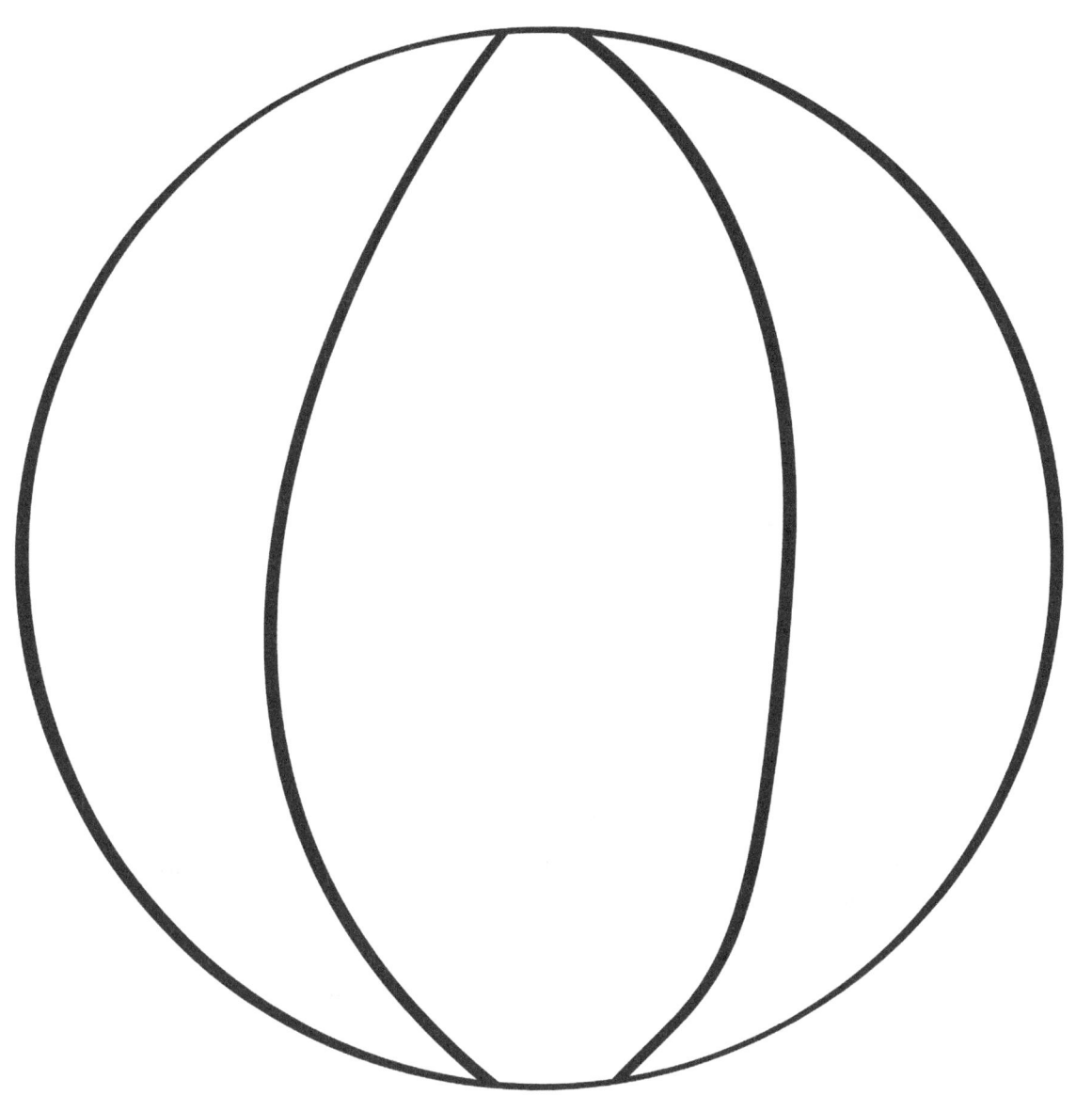

Portal

We choose one portal of experience and listen for a truth emanating from within. Perhaps we hear it best when it is echoed from the space in which we find ourselves. Passing through any particular gateway to experience, we may see ourselves in a different light and be opened to new understandings of who we are and why we move through space and time.

SEEDS Journaling Practice: *Soul Activation Quest-ions to Consider*

- From your current chosen portal of experience, do you hear or see mysteries from beyond? What truths echo here? Are they resonant with your soul's deepest knowing?

- What or where are your sacred spaces? What are your thin places where Spirit moves easily through your life?

- What are the portals in space and time or the gateways to experience through which you have already passed? What truths have emerged? Who do you now know yourself to be, having passed that way once upon a time?

- Gazing into your interpretation of this SEA doodle, what questions arise from within? Record them here and explore further.

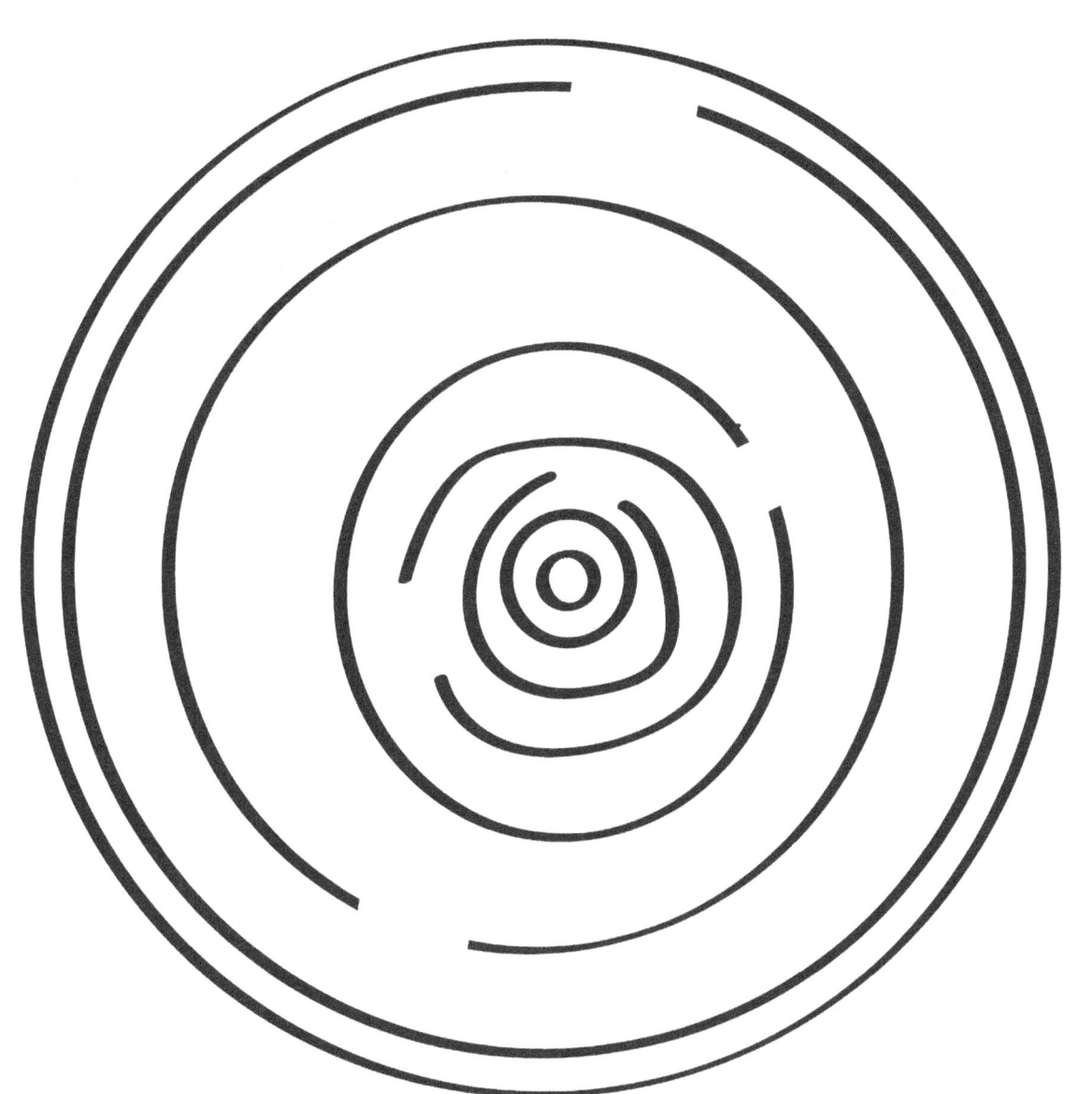

Quickening

The pace of our lives may quicken at various points along our life's essential journey. While it may seem we are moving round and round and not much is happening, this cycle of change may hold new dimensions of experience. We are stretched. Our muscles grow strong. We find our footing and move on.

SEEDS Journaling Practice: *Soul Activation Quest-ions to Consider*

➡ How are you picking up the pace? What is happening as you move through life? Beneath the accelerated steps, what might be calling out for your soul's attention?

➡ What if you stopped for a moment to pause and consider? Have you outgrown the circle in which you find yourself or is there yet room to grow within it? How might you play with a new rhythm for your life?

➡ How is your present experience changing you? How are you being stretched? How does this feel? How might you tend to your soul and water your life with love as you move within this sphere of being?

➡ Gazing into your interpretation of this SEA doodle, what questions arise from within? Record them here and explore further.

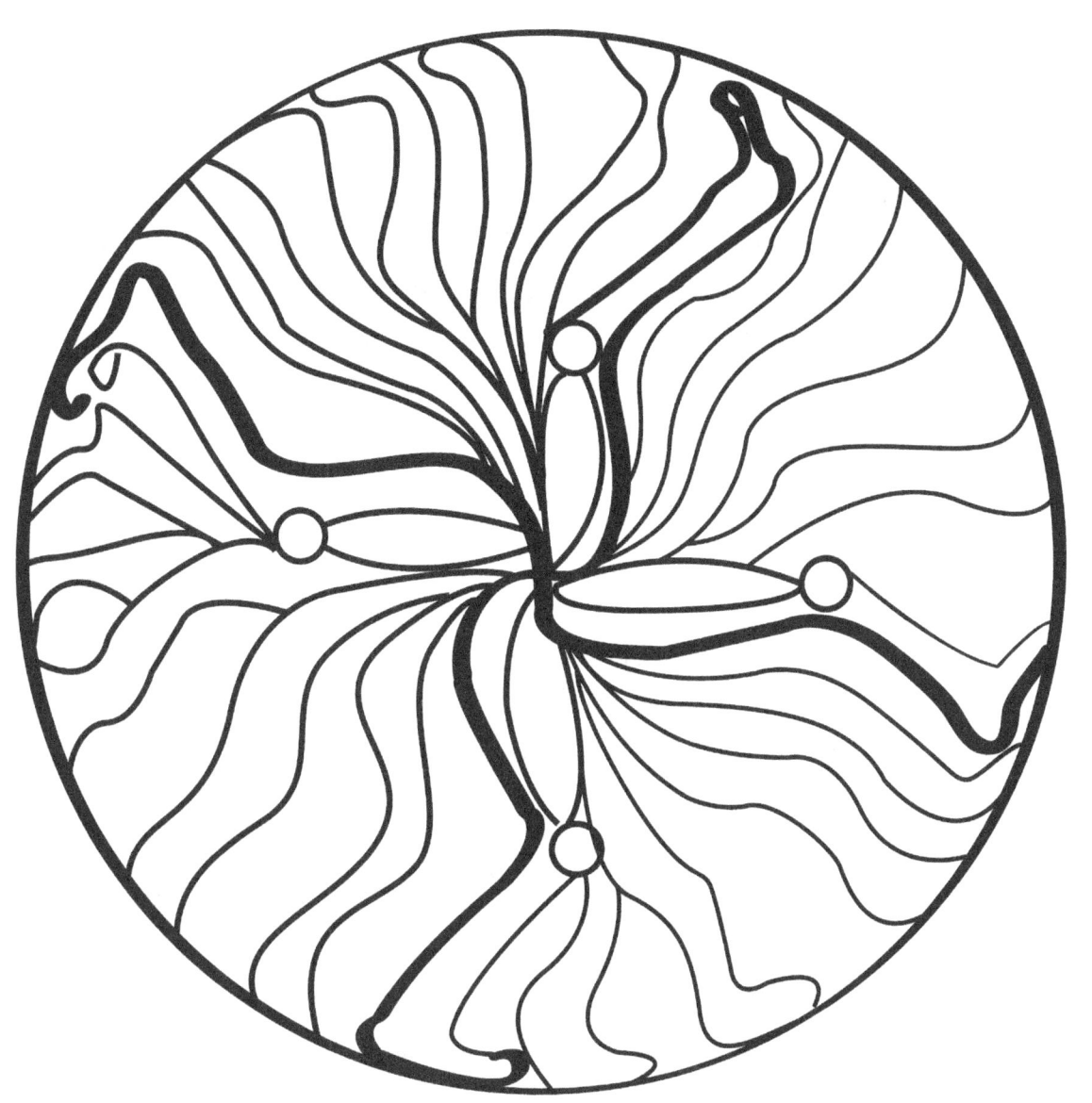

Reach of Love

Love is someone you are. When you know yourself as love, you may reach within to express its rainbow hope and share the seed of that experience with another. All the while, the love you are expands in energetic waves of grace that reach to the heavens and to the watery depths. Poured out, your life becomes a ministry of reconciliation, and the reach of love is infinite.

SEEDS Journaling Practice: *Soul Activation Quest-ions to Consider*

- Do you see yourself as love? Consider all the ways you know love to be the foundation of who you are. If you do not see yourself as love, where do you see the reach of love in the world around you?

- Do you feel safe in space and time? Do you imagine a banner of love and a circle of care with you now and always? How do you feel the gracious protection of love as you move from day to day? If you do not feel that love, how might you look for love today?

- How have the gifts of love and moments of presence you have shared with another seeded the reach of love? How has love changed a situation, enriched the life of another, or come back to change your own?

- Gazing into your interpretation of this SEA doodle, what questions arise from within? Record them here and explore further.

Receptacle

We are beings filled with life, lighted by truth, and set upon our way. When we open to life to receive and willingly share what nourishment we have to offer, water is turned to wine and life itself transforms. Each one of us is a sacred cup of mystery, a chalice filled to the brim with sweet drops of life. We are invited now to hold sacred these life-giving waters and the cup that is ours to share.

SEEDS Journaling Practice: *Soul Activation Quest-ions to Consider*

- How is your life a receptacle?
- Are you remaining open, willing to be filled with more light, life, and love?
- Do you feel there are angels or a divine presence with you as you journey through this life? What is the role they fulfill? How are these guardians assisting you in protecting sacred treasure?
- Gazing into your interpretation of this SEA doodle, what questions arise from within? Record them here and explore further.

Spatial Dimensions

We look and see the shape of our lives, but we forget we are seeing from a single vantage point. Within the shape we see are infinite varieties of design, sacred patterns of originality that activate and awaken others just because we are. As we explore new ideas and ways of exploring, expressing, and expanding from the whole within, we are, through the very process of our engagement with our lives, offering that same gift to others.

SEEDS Journaling Practice: *Soul Activation Quest-ions to Consider*

- How does your life look different when viewed from a different perspective? Where are the surfaces and what is reflected through the prism of your life's current field of experience?

- What are you waiting for? Pick a point, any point, and begin to explore your soul and be the agent of change you were born to be by the very act of beginning and beginning again.

- When you consider your current life's experience, what is the shape that comes to mind? What gift does this shape have to offer you?

- Gazing into your interpretation of this SEA doodle, what questions arise from within? Record them here and explore further.

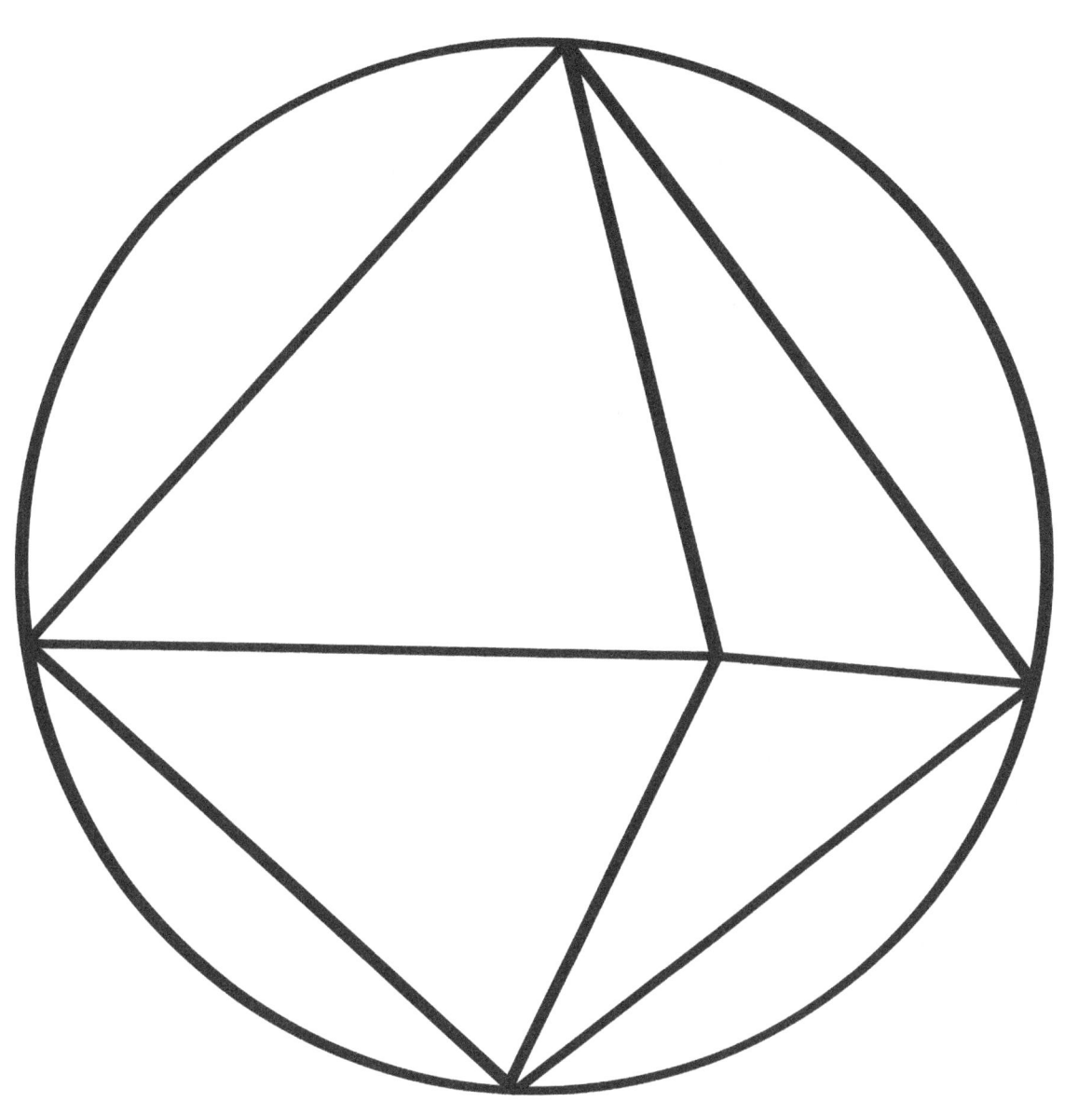

Speak Faith

If the faith of a small seed might move mountains, what might your choice to speak faith about your own life do? Listen to your life. Choose to speak words that affirm it and celebrate its course, and watch the joy of a whole new world being born unto itself. Then, smile and move forward in confidence, certain that life is working in your favor. Love will meet you on your way.

SEEDS Journaling Practice: *Soul Activation Quest-ions to Consider*

➡ It has been written, "Out of the treasures of the heart the mouth speaks." What words do you speak that might remind you of the true treasure which you hold?

➡ In the multiplying voices, have you lost your own? How might you return to the still center point and know that you are?

➡ Is it hard to hear the "still, small voice" of your own life's truth? How might you let your life speak?

➡ Gazing into your interpretation of this SEA doodle, what questions arise from within? Record them here and explore further.

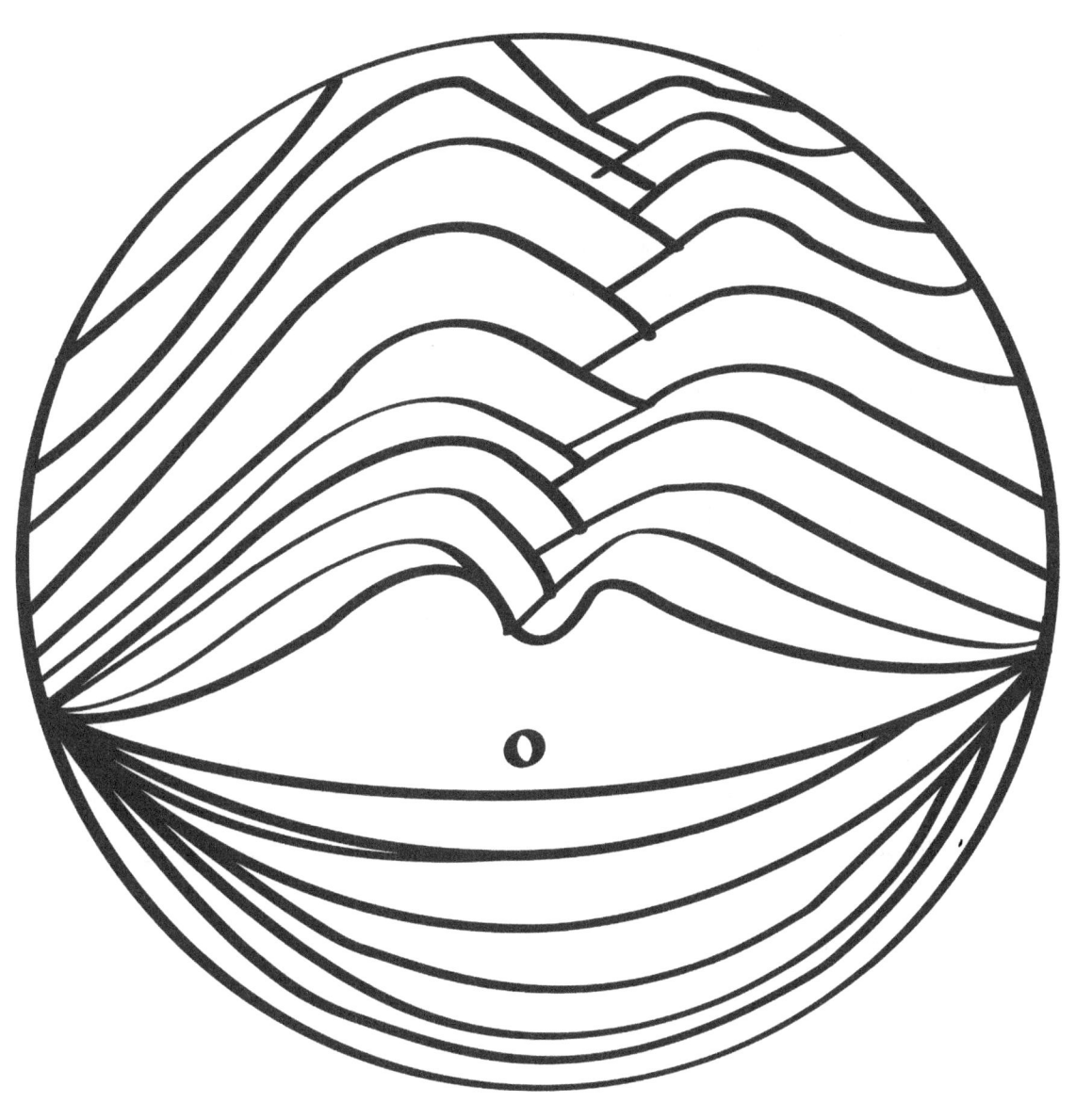

The Mountain and Me

There will come a day when you will find yourself blocked, mountains standing in your way. Perhaps there will be a fissure in the ground you thought so sure. Or every way through will seem to be closed. Stand and see. Reach within to learn something new about who you are. Then turn toward the mountain and hear her voice calling you to greater heights, whether attained by making the climb or moving in a new direction.

SEEDS Journaling Practice: *Soul Activation Quest-ions to Consider*

➡ Are you the mountain that needs to move? Where in your life are you getting in your own way?

➡ How are you ready for a new perspective? Survey the landscape in which you feel lost or blocked from forward progress. Ask the hills and mountains to share their wisdom. Listen to what they seem to say to you.

➡ Ask to be shown a whole new way forward in this present circumstance.

➡ Gazing into your interpretation of this SEA doodle, what questions arise from within? Record them here and explore further.

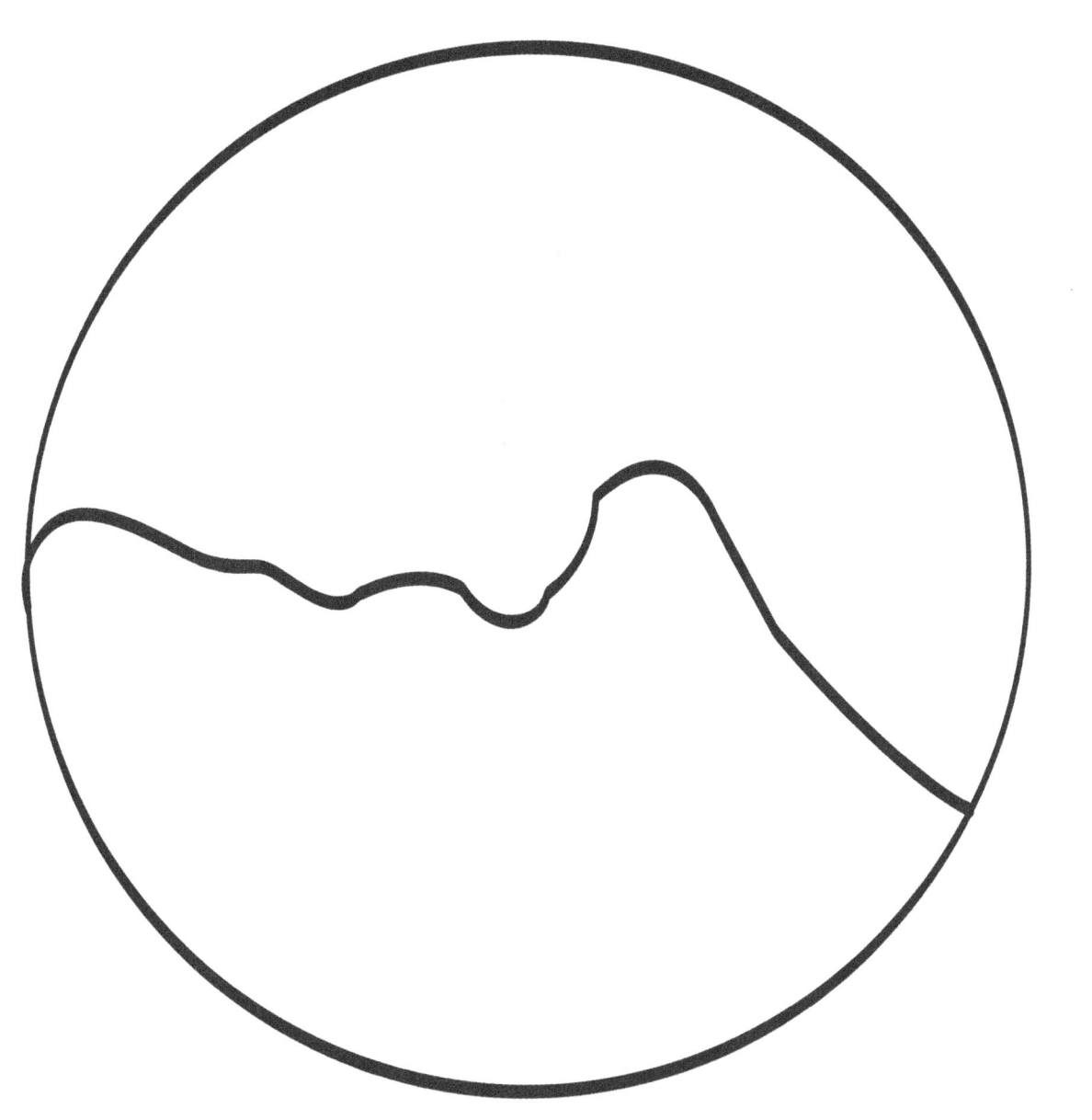

Threefold Love

A great love runs through life and makes its way to infinite varieties of expression. Three expressions may come together to represent a single shining truth. These triads offer a whole new way of seeing who we are, of being who we are, and of freeing who we are. Through the lens of this multidimensional experience, we play with the patterns of our life and begin to imagine a larger life than the one at first we thought ourselves to be living.

SEEDS Journaling Practice: *Soul Activation Quest-ions to Consider*

➡ What three qualities or expressions of great love are sustaining you? Do you see the ways these expressions of love become interwoven and expand your life?

➡ What unique perspective is offered where two of the three come together? What is the opportunity to find yourself at these points of convergence and be born to something new?

➡ How might you step into each of these three expressions of love and join each, receiving full its gifts and sharing the bounty of blessing with others through this particular lens of experience?

➡ Gazing into your interpretation of this SEA doodle, what questions arise from within? Record them here and explore further.

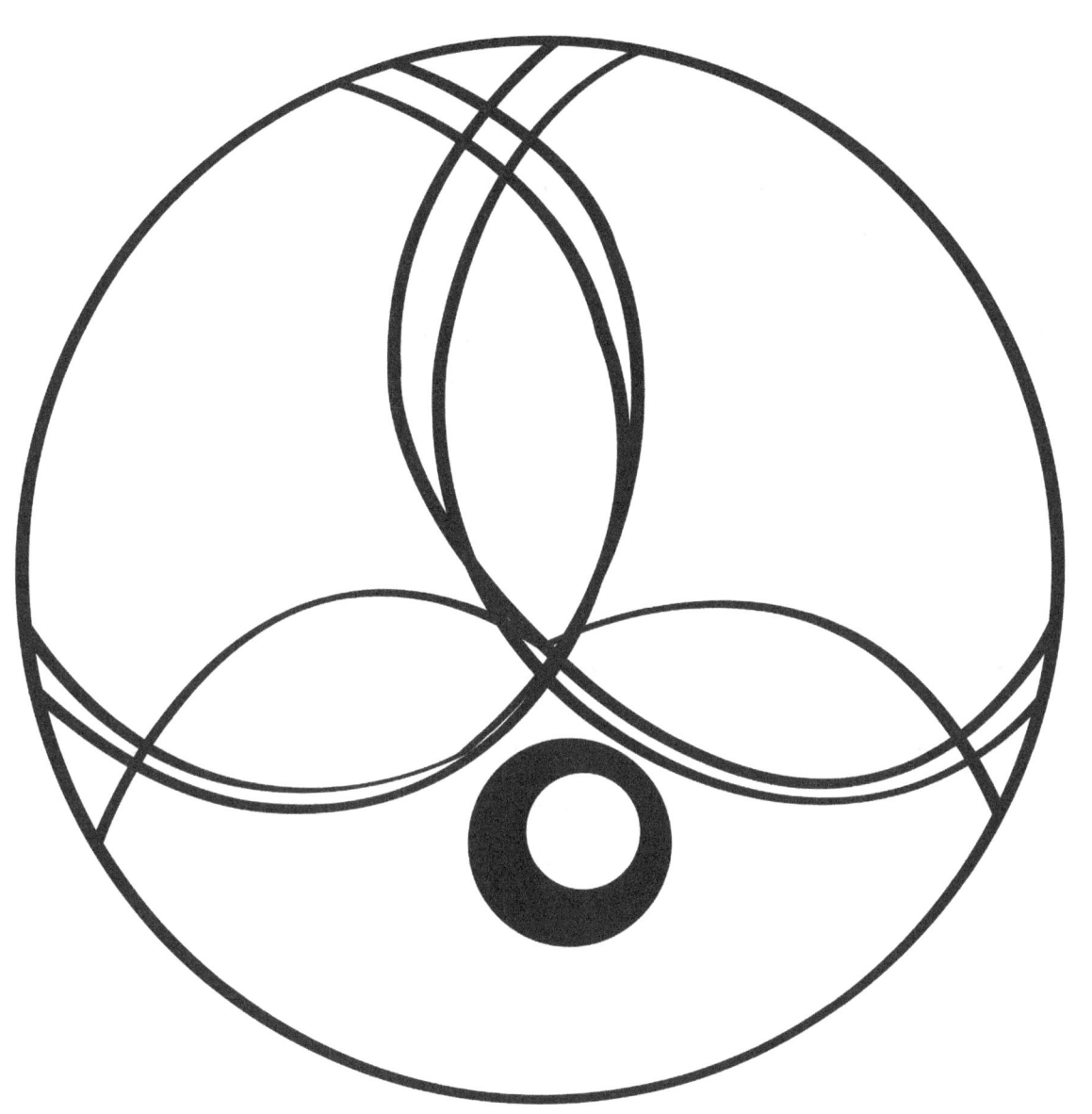

Time Dimensions

Our experience of ourselves is influenced here by time, yet we see time as flat and ordinary. What if there were something more here to be experienced? As you enter into each new segment of time as it is operating in our world, bring yourself fully here and now. At the same time, step into a whole new perspective of the "you" who exists in the All That Is, beyond the reach of time.

SEEDS Journaling Practice: *Soul Activation Quest-ions to Consider*

➡ In time's turning, how do you change? How do you stay the same?

➡ What if time moved in all directions? What if it expanded in response to all you bring into it? Consider new definitions of time. Consider how you might build greater trust and know you have all the time you need.

➡ What timeless truths do you hold sacred in this time and space?

➡ Gazing into your interpretation of this SEA doodle, what questions arise from within? Record them here and explore further.

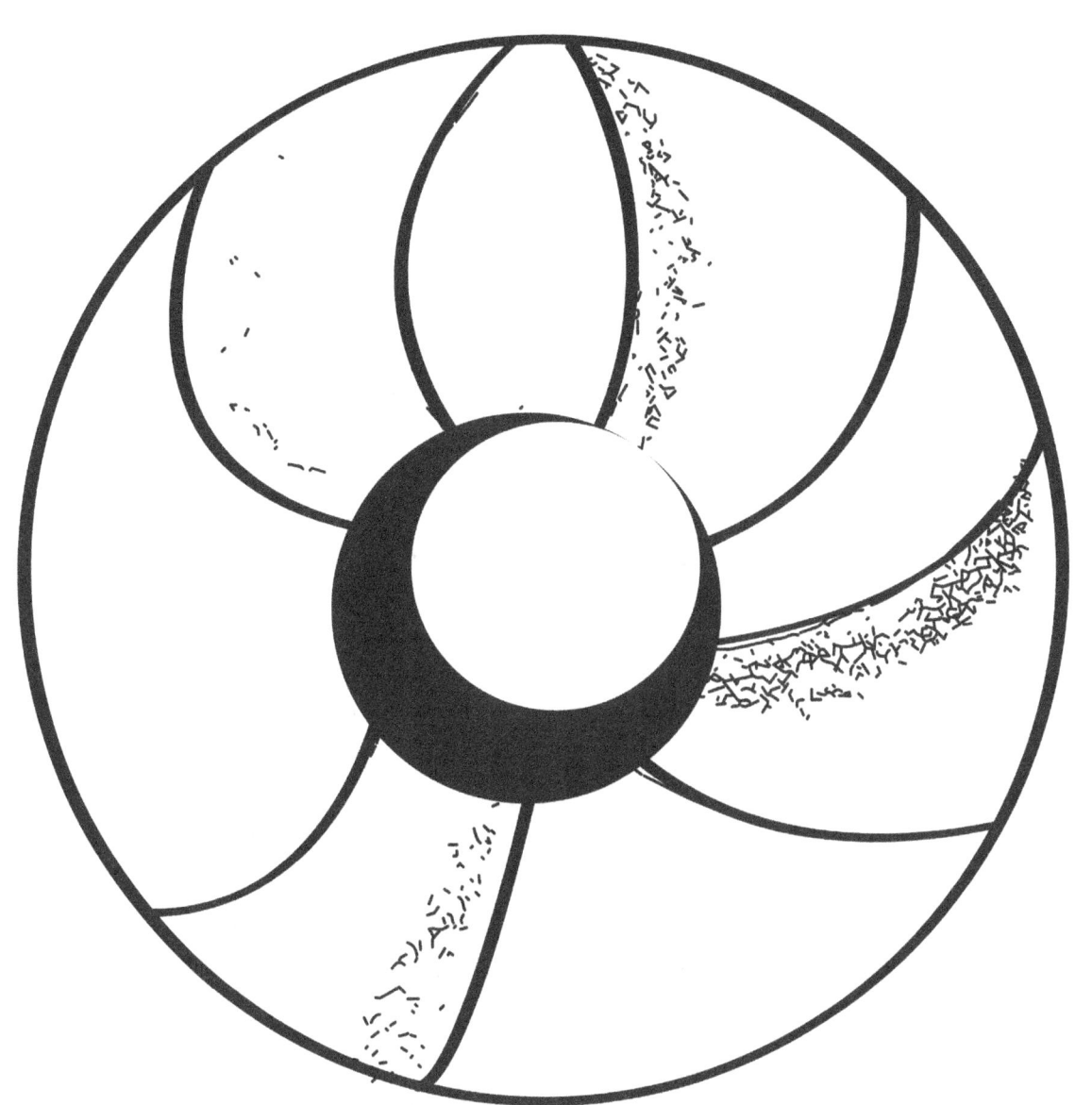

Tropical Truth

Where all things are equal and at rest for you uniquely, there is peace. There is rest and restoration. There, in that place of knowing what you know, is the entrance to a tropical paradise and heaven on Earth. That entrance is in the center, in your soul, on the line that never ends. It is from this place of beauty that light breaks forth and life spills forth as a river wild. It is here, within the whole of creation you are, that love is born.

SEEDS Journaling Practice: *Soul Activation Quest-ions to Consider*

- What two twirling dervishes live inside of you? What are the truths they would invite you to consider? How are these truths two expressions of a single, unified field of knowing?

- How do we know whose reflection is true? Can we trust what we see? How might the contrasting reflections of truth lead us back to our soul's resting place, where all is well?

- Do you know what I know? Would you share what essential truth you have found as you have walked ten thousand proverbial miles only to arrive back where it all began?

- Gazing into your interpretation of this SEA doodle, what questions arise from within? Record them here and explore further.

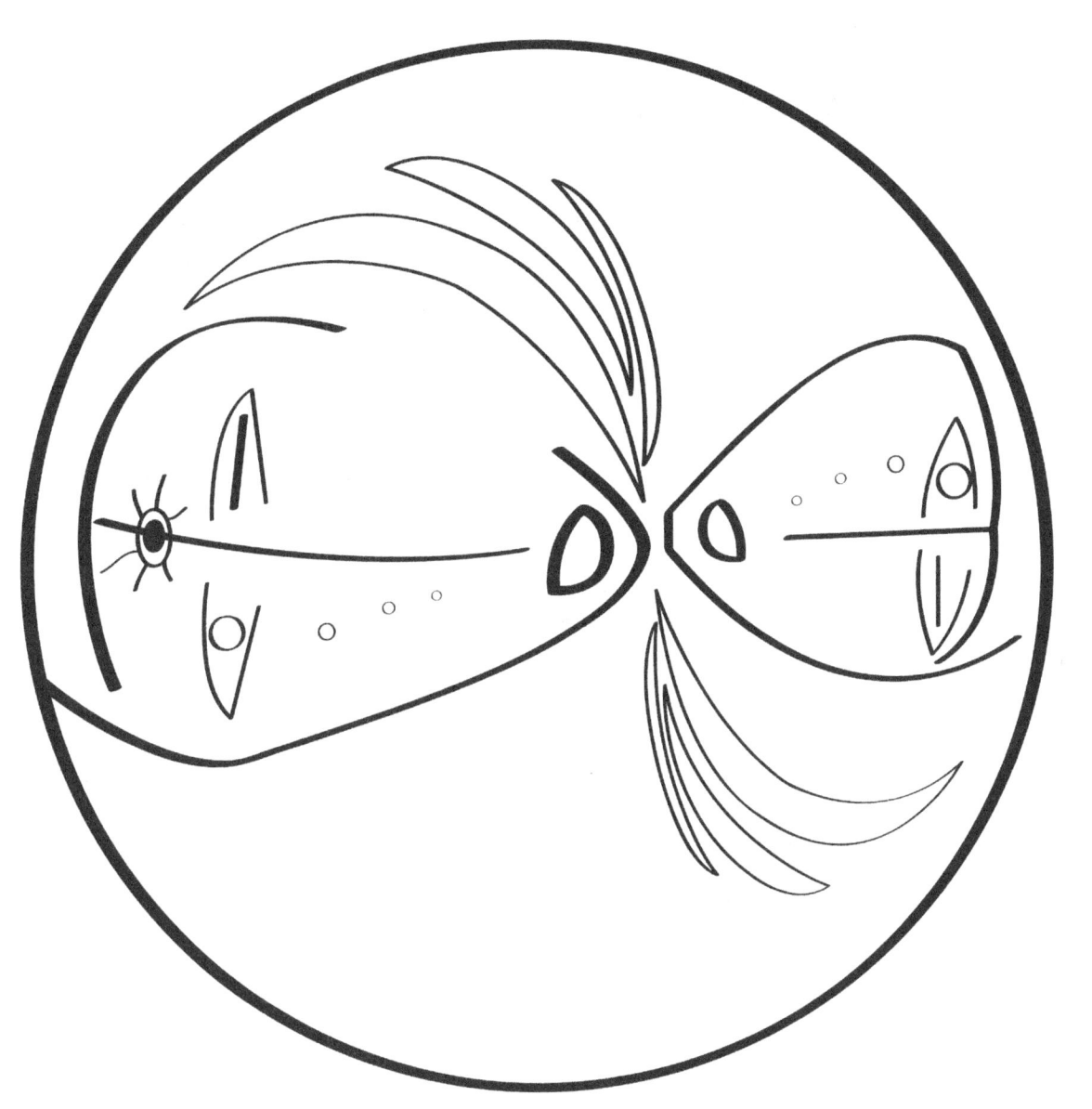

Unexpected Opportunity

We pass through the same door again and again, entering into a familiar experience. But life surprises us, and the world expands. Expect the unexpected as you make the journey of a soul and live into this singularly magnificent story of your life.

SEEDS Journaling Practice: *Soul Activation Quest-ions to Consider*

- Write a series of love notes to remind you to dance your chance when the opportunity arises to say, "Yes!" to new experience.

- How might you look for opportunity by walking along the edge? Looking from the inside out? Stepping outside your comfort zone?

- Can there really ever be a missed opportunity? What practices will you adopt to bring a greater awareness to what is possible in the shape of your here and now? How will you step into what might be?

- Gazing into your interpretation of this SEA doodle, what questions arise from within? Record them here and explore further.

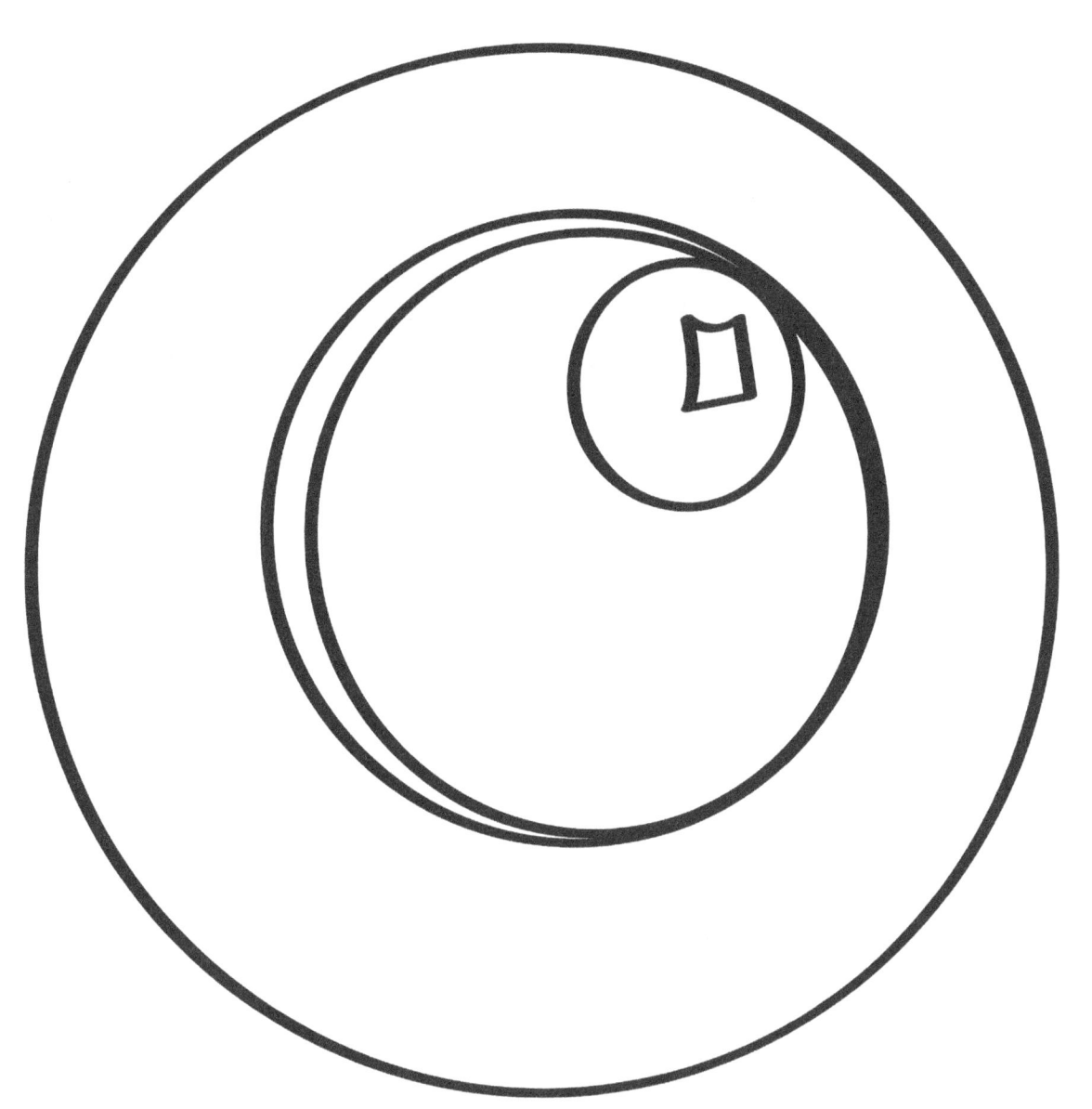

Universal

There is the personal energy we bring to life, our unique soul signature and the gifts we bring. There is also at our core a universal energy that flows through us and emanates from us when we receive its gift to us. These two work in tandem, the one illuminating the other. The universal dance of life is an invitation to experience them both fully and move to pass these gifts to another.

SEEDS Journaling Practice: *Soul Activation Quest-ions to Consider*

- How will you hold the universe in you? How might you share this universal energy with others and trust the unbreakable bonds that keep your soul intact?

- In what ways does your unique soul signature attract others to you? What are they most curious to know? How might you share your unique life energy?

- As you explore and grow, what are those things that might hook you or restrain you? How can you choose to swim free but remain connected to the life-force energy that is the foundation of your soul?

- Gazing into your interpretation of this SEA doodle, what questions arise from within? Record them here and explore further.

Woman, River

Life flows through you and flows forth from you as you come current and stand in the streams of your soul. Life grows in you and grows from you as you surrender all resistance to its flow and allow. Find your forward flow as you celebrate your point of origin and originality and release the light and life and love you are, knowing it will not and cannot be extinguished or consumed. You are a river, a woman born to life again and again and again.

SEEDS Journaling Practice: *Soul Activation Quest-ions to Consider*

- How is the woman you would be calling out to you? Listen beneath the rushing currents and the babbling all around. What does she say?
- How will you choose to birth every moment and be born to it?
- How do you give and receive life by bringing yourself to the full reclamation and radiant realization of the whole of who you are as a woman? As a river flowing through time? As a bearer of light, a bringer of life, and a banner of love?
- Gazing into your interpretation of this SEA doodle, what questions arise from within? Record them here and explore further.

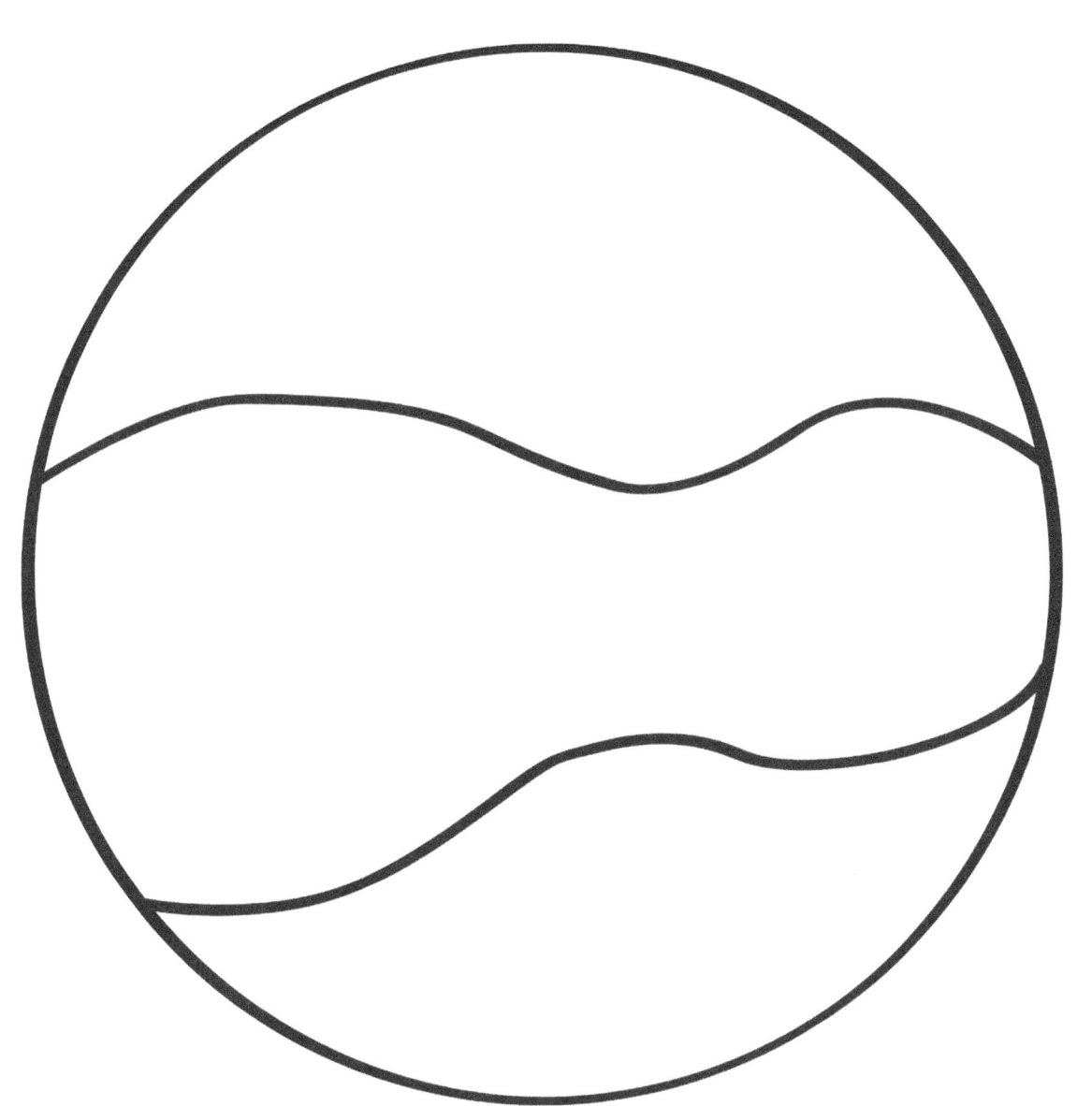

Books by This Author

Visit DawnRicherson.com

Cultivating Essence from the Matrix of Soul
Awakening the World Within
Finding Our Forward Flow
Embracing a New Vision

Seeds for Life
Birds of a Feather
All Systems Go

True Identity
A Reconciliation of Light
12 Doors of Abundance
Energetic Perspectives

Journey to the Heartland
Journey to Sacred Wholeness
Sacred Partnership

Many Rivers Flow
Across the Seas of Time
Testament: A Half-Life in Poems
The Magda Poems

From the Heart of a Child
To Sin by Silence

www.ingramcontent.com/pod-product-compliance
Lightning Source LLC
Chambersburg PA
CBHW081502070526
44586CB00019B/2457